AGES
5-6
Key Stage 1

Reading Practice

Bath · New York · Cologne · Melbourne · Delhi
Hong Kong · Shenzhen · Singapore

Helping your child

⭐ The activities in this book will help your child to develop their reading skills.

⭐ Your child will gain confidence in sounding out individual words and reading a range of poems, stories and non-fiction texts.

⭐ Your child will learn about blending sounds, begin to recognize words with different endings, identify rhyming words and explore the meaning of words. Your child will also begin to read texts for meaning and answer comprehension questions.

⭐ Set aside time to do the activities together. Do a little at a time so that your child enjoys learning. Read the instructions and texts with them.

⭐ Give lots of encouragement and praise. Use the gold stars as rewards and incentives.

⭐ The answers are on page 32.

This edition published by Parragon Books Ltd in 2016

Parragon Books Ltd
Chartist House
15-17 Trim Street
Bath BA1 1HA, UK
www.parragon.com

Copyright © Parragon Books Ltd 2002–2016

Written by Nina Filipek and Catherine Casey
Illustrated by Simon Abbot and Adam Linley
Educational Consultant: Geraldine Taylor

All rights reserved. No part of this publication may be reproduced, stored in a retrieval system or transmitted, in any form or by any means, electronic, mechanical, photocopying, recording or otherwise, without the prior permission of the copyright holder.

ISBN 978-1-4748-4738-4

Printed in China

Contents

Match the words	4
Find the sounds	6
Choose the correct word	7
Words ending in **s** and **es**	8
Words ending in **ed** and **ing**	9
Words ending in **er** and **est**	10
Understanding syllables	11
Missing letters	12
Useful words	13
Word meanings	14
Rhyming words	15
Read a poem	16
Read a story	18
Your favourite story	20
Yes or no	21
Read instructions	22
Traditional tales	24
Book titles	26
Story openings	27
Making predictions	28
Making sense	30
Answers	32

Match the words

Read the descriptions in the boxes below. Draw a ring around the description that matches each picture.

a brown hat

a brown hen

a pink dress

a pink press

a bare foot

a bare boat

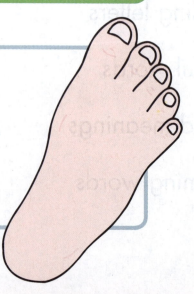

Note for parent: This activity helps your child to blend phonemes (sounds) to decode words. Phonemes are the smallest units of sound and there are over 40 used in English.

an orange box ✗

an orange fox —

a shiny crown —

a shiny clown

a slow snail —

a slow bird

Find the sounds

Draw a line to match each word to the correct sound that is in the word. The first one has been done for you. There are two words for each sound.

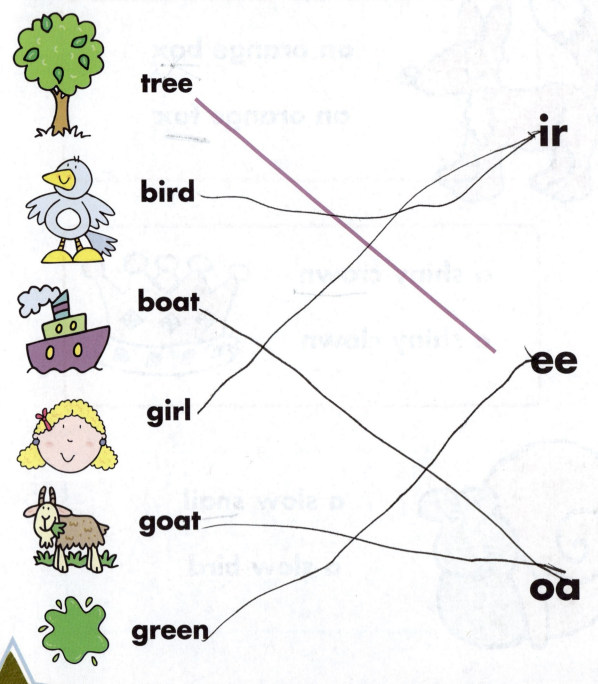

Note for parent: A digraph is two letters that make one sounds. For example: oo, oa, ai, ee, ue and or.

Choose the correct word

Read the sentences below. Look at the picture and choose the correct word to complete each sentence. Write the words on the lines.

Jane has a warm ~~coa~~ coat.

coat / cat

I read a book.

book / boat

The train is green.

blue / green

The farmer has a horse.

sheep / horse

Note for parent: You could underline or circle the digraph in each word together with your child.

Words ending in s and es

Read the sentence about Adam below.

Adam plays with a ball.

Read the sentences below. Choose the correct word to complete each sentence. Write the words on the lines.

| washes | reads | plays |

Harry _reads_ a book.

Omar _washes_ the car.

Layla _plays_ tennis.

Words ending in ed and ing

Read these sentences to see how they are different.

The lion is roaring.
↓
This is happening.

The lion roared.
↓
This has happened.

Read the sentences below. Choose the correct word to complete each sentence. Write the words on the lines.

| hissed | barked | jumped |

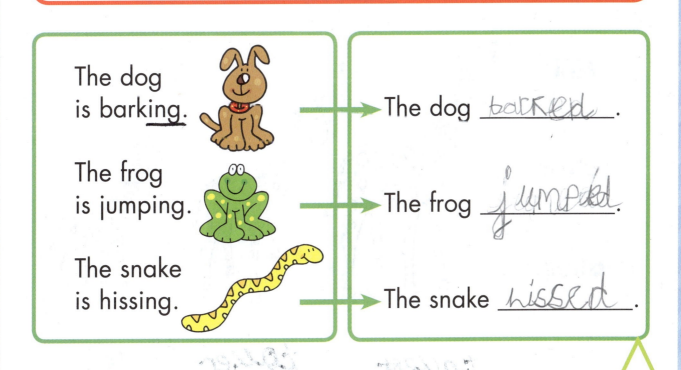

The dog is barking. → The dog _barked_.

The frog is jumping. → The frog _jumped_.

The snake is hissing. → The snake _hissed_.

Note for parent: Explain to your child that words ending in -ing show that an action is happening and words ending in -ed show that an action has already happened.

Read the words in the boxes. Choose the correct word to match each picture and write it in the space below.

big

bigger

biggest

big   *bigger*   *biggest*

tall

taller

tallest

tallest   *taller*   tall

Note for parent: Help your child to think of some other words that have -er and -est endings. For example: long and strong.

Understanding syllables

A syllable is the part of a word that sounds like a beat as we say the word. Try reading these words.

> **el-e-phant   di-no-saur   ro-bot**
> **rab-bit   ba-na-na   car-rot**

Read the sentences below. Look at the picture and choose the correct word to complete each sentence. Write the words on the lines.

The book was about a _dinosaur_.

elephant / dinosaur

 The _robot_ was big and blue.

rabbit / robot

The rabbit ate a _carrot_.

banana / carrot

Missing letters

We sometimes combine two words into one word. When we write the new word, we use an apostrophe to show where the missing spaces and letters should be.

For example:

I am = I'm   **I will = I'll**

Follow the lines to match each set of words to the correct shortened word.

I will   **didn't**

did not   **I'll**

we will   **don't**

do not   **we'll**

Note for parent: These shortened words are called 'contractions'. Try to think of some more contractions with your child. For example: can not = can't, has not = hasn't.

Useful words

Some words are not easy to read by blending the sounds of the letters. You need to learn these words by memory. See if you can remember these useful words:

the	said	once	she
you	was	they	
are	come	his	time

Can you spot any of the words above in the story below? Draw a ring around each word in the story.

Once upon a time there lived a king.

He was very sad. He had lost his crown.

The queen was kind.

She said: "You are OK. Come on, let's look for it."

They found it in the garden.

Word meanings

Read the sentences below. Choose the correct word to match each description. Write the words on the lines and draw pictures of the words in the boxes. The first one has been done for you.

astronaut   moon   rocket

A person who works in space.

astronaut

A spacecraft that travels into space.

Rocket

A round or crescent shape that shines in the sky at night.

moon

Rhyming words

Read the words. Draw a line to match each word to its rhyming pair. The first one has been done for you.

Read the poem below. Find the rhyming words at the end of the lines. Trace over each pair of rhyming words with the same coloured pen.

Twinkle, Twinkle, Little Star

Twinkle, twinkle, little star,

How I wonder what you are!

Up above the world so high,

Like a diamond in the sky.

When the blazing sun is gone,

When it nothing shines upon,

Then you show your little light,

Twinkle, twinkle, all the night.

Read the sentences below. Choose the correct word to complete each sentence. Draw a ring around the correct answer.

The little star looked like a...
dog / diamond

The little star is...
up above / down below
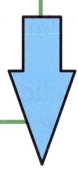

The little star appears...
at night / in the day

Read a story

Read the story below.

Bella's Bedtime

It was Bella's bedtime, but she couldn't find Bertie Bear and she didn't want to go to sleep without him.

She looked on the bedroom floor, in the toy box and under the bed.

"I'm sure we'll find him tomorrow," said Mum.

Bella wiped away her tears and pulled back the bedcover.

Bertie was fast asleep on her pillow!

Read the sentences below. Choose the correct word to complete each sentence. Draw a ring around each correct answer.

At the beginning of the story Bella couldn't find…

her shoes **Bertie Bear**

Bella looked for Bertie Bear in the…

bedroom **bathroom**

Mum said that they would…

buy another bear **find him tomorrow**

Your favourite story

What is your favourite story or book?
Draw a picture of it in the space below.

Note for parent: In this activity your child is exploring how to express their personal opinions about things they have read.

Yes or no

Read the sentences. Look at the picture and decide whether each sentence matches the picture. Write **yes** or **no** on the lines.

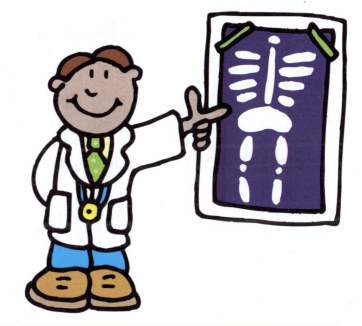

The doctor is pointing at an x-ray. _____

The doctor is wearing a red tie. _____

You can see bones in an x-ray. _____

The doctor is happy with the x-ray. _____

Read instructions

Read the instructions below. Follow the instructions to colour in the clothes correctly.

1. Colour both the socks in with red and blue stripes.

2. Colour one t-shirt in yellow and the other in green.

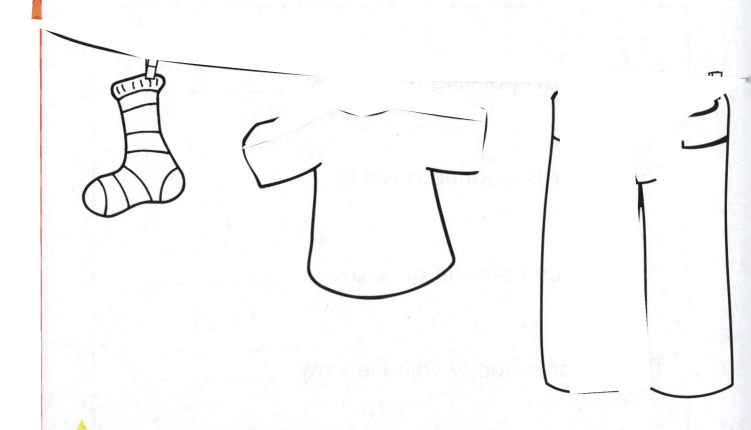

Note for parent: In this activity, your child needs to understand what they have read in order to complete the activity.

3. Colour the trousers on the end in blue.

4. Colour the trousers in the middle in red.

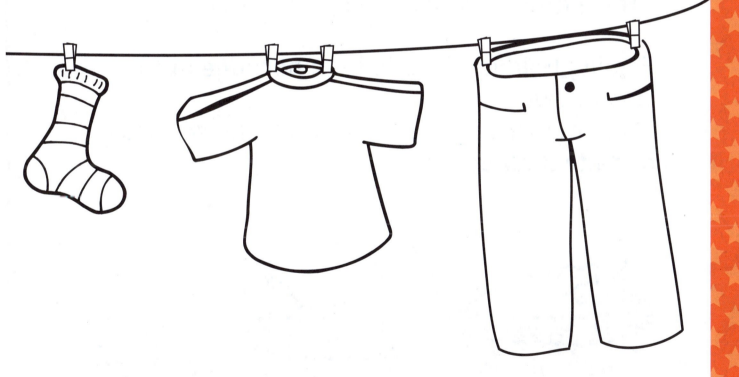

Traditional tales

Read this passage from a traditional fairy tale.

Goldilocks and the Three Bears

Goldilocks tasted the porridge in the big bowl.
"This porridge is too salty," she said.

Then Goldilocks tasted the porridge in the medium bowl.
"This porridge is too sweet," she said.

Finally, Goldilocks tasted the porridge in the small bowl.
"Yummy! This porridge is just right," she said, and ate it all up.

Read the sentences in the boxes below. Choose the correct word to complete each sentence. Write the words on the lines.

big   medium   small

The porridge in the _____ bowl was too sweet.

The porridge in the _____ bowl was too salty.

The porridge in the _____ bowl was just right.

Can you retell the passage in your own words?
_____
_____
_____
_____
_____

Read the book titles. Underline the title that is the best match for each book cover.

Merlin's Magical Day

Willow Witch Goes on Holiday

Baby Parrot has a Party

Baby Owl Likes the Dark

Danny the Happy Dinosaur

Scary Dinosaur on the Run

Story openings

Read the story openings. Underline each set of words that match the pictures.

Once upon a time there were…

three bunnies

three bears

Long, long ago there lived a…

kind king

quiet queen

Once upon a time there was a…

witch called Wanda

boat called Wanda

Making predictions

Read the sentences. Predict the missing words to complete the story. Write the words on the lines.

The Enormous Turnip

One day Dad planted some turnip seeds.

One grew bigger than all the others.

It grew bigger and _____ and bigger until it was enormous!

Dad pulled the enormous turnip. But he couldn't pull it up.

Dad asked Mum, Tom and Tilly to help.

Mum pulled the turnip.

Tom _____ the turnip.

Tilly _____ the turnip.

What do you think happens next in the story? Draw what you think happens next in the box below.

Read the sentences. Cross out the silly word in each sentence. Look at the picture and choose the correct word to replace each silly word. Write the words on the lines.

bread   brother's   stool

I had paper for breakfast.

_____

It's my flower's birthday today.

_____

I sat on the blue school.

_____

| chocolate | sunny | coat | shopping |

I bought a warm pencil for winter.

_____

The weather is very fluffy today.

_____

I love wooden ice-cream.

_____

I like swimming in the supermarket.

_____

Pages 4–5
a brown hen
a pink dress
a bare foot
an orange fox
a shiny crown
a slow snail

Page 6
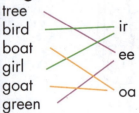
tree — ee
bird — ir
boat — oa
girl — ir
goat — oa
green — ee

Page 7
Jane has a warm **coat**.
I read a **book**.
The train is **green**.
The farmer has a **horse**.

Page 8
Harry **reads** a book.
Omar **washes** the car.
Layla **plays** tennis.

Page 9
The dog **barked**.
The frog **jumped**.
The snake **hissed**.

Page 10
big, bigger, biggest
tallest, taller, tall

Page 11
The book was about a **dinosaur**.
The **robot** was big and blue.
The rabbit ate a **carrot**.

Page 12
I will → I'll
did not → didn't
we will → we'll
do not → don't

Page 13
Once upon a **time**
there lived a king.
He **was** very sad.
He had lost **his** crown.
The queen **was** kind.
She said: "**You are** OK.
Come on, let's look for it."
They found it in **the** garden.

Page 14
astronaut, rocket, moon

Page 15
bat / hat
day / say
top / hop
tree / three

Page 16
star / are
high / sky
gone / upon
light / night

Page 17
The little star looked like a…
diamond
The little star is…
up above
The little star appears…
at night

Page 19
At the beginning of the story Bella couldn't find…
Bertie Bear
Bella looked for Bertie Bear in the…
bedroom
Mum said that they would…
find him tomorrow

Page 21
yes, no, yes, yes

Pages 22–23

Page 25
The porridge in the **medium** bowl was too sweet.
The porridge in the **big** bowl was too salty.
The porridge in the **small** bowl was just right.

Page 26
Merlin's Magical Day
Baby Owl Likes the Dark
Danny the Happy Dinosaur

Page 27
Once upon a time there were… **three bears**
Long, long ago there lived a… **kind king**
Once upon a time there was a… **witch called Wanda**

Page 28
It grew bigger and **bigger** and bigger until it was enormous!
Tom **pulled** the turnip.
Tilly **pulled** the turnip.

Pages 30–31
bread, brother's, stool, coat, sunny, chocolate, shopping